Pebble
Plus

Great White Sharks

by Deborah Nuzzolo

CAPSTONE PRESS
a capstone imprint

Pebble Plus is published by Capstone Press,
1710 Roe Crest Drive, North Mankato, Minnesota 56003
www.mycapstone.com

Library of Congress Cataloging-in-Publication Data
Names: Nuzzolo, Deborah, author.
Title: Great white sharks / by Deborah Nuzzolo.
Description: North Mankato, Minnesota : Capstone Press, [2017] | Series:
 Pebble plus. All about sharks | Audience: Ages 4–8. | Audience: K to grade 3. |
Includes bibliographical references and index.
Identifiers: LCCN 2016059065 | ISBN 9781515770022 (library binding) |
ISBN 9781515770084 (pbk.) | ISBN 9781515770145 (ebook (pdf))
Subjects: LCSH: White shark—Juvenile literature. | CYAC: Sharks.
Classification: LCC QL638.95.L3 B347 2018 | DDC 597.3/3—dc23
LC record available at https://lccn.loc.gov/2016059065]

Editorial Credits
Nikki Bruno Clapper, editor; Kayla Rossow, designer;
Kelly Garvin, media researcher; Gene Bentdahl, production specialist

Photo Credits
Getty Images/Premium UIG, 19; Seapics/C & M Fallows, 15; Shutterstock: Alessandro De Maddalena, 11,
Grant Henderson, 13, Joe Belanger, 1, Modens Trolle, 17, nirtogenic.com, 7, Palomba, 9, Rich Carey, 2, 24,
Sergey Uryadnikov, 5, VisionDive, cover, wildestanimal, 21, Willyam Bradberry, 23

Artistic elements
Shutterstock: Apostrophe, HorenkO, Magenta10

Note to Parents and Teachers

The All About Sharks set supports national curriculum standards for science related
to the characteristics and behavior of animals. This book describes and illustrates
great white sharks. The images support early readers in understanding the text.
The repetition of words and phrases helps early readers learn new words. This book
also introduces early readers to subject-specific vocabulary words, which are defined
in the Glossary section. Early readers may need assistance to read some words and
to use the Table of Contents, Glossary, Read More, Internet Sites, Critical Thinking
Questions, and Index sections of the book.

Printed in China.
004704

Table of Contents

A Leap and a Bite

A large shark sees a seal

near the ocean's surface.

Zoom! The shark races upward.

It leaps into the air

and catches the seal.

Great white sharks are the largest hunting fish in the world. They live in mostly cool seas.

5 feet (1.5 meters)

15 feet (4.6 meters)

A Football-Shaped Fish

A great white's body looks like a long football. This shape helps the shark speed through the water.

A great white shark is
not all white. It has a gray
back and a white belly.
The gray color blends in
with the ocean floor.

Great whites have a nostril on each side of their snout. They use their nostrils to smell prey. Great whites can smell blood from far away.

nostrils

Hunting and Eating

Great white sharks hunt seals,

sea lions, and small whales.

A big meal can feed one of these

sharks for more than a month.

A great white shark's jaws hold about 300 sharp teeth. Few animals can escape its jaws.

Great White Babies

Great white shark pups are born live. Between 2 and 10 pups are born at one time. The pups are about 5 feet (1.5 meters) long.

The pups leave their mother right away. Young great whites live on their own. These sharks can live for more than 30 years.

Glossary

escape—to get away from

hunt—to find and catch animals for food

nostril—one of the two outside openings in the nose used to breathe and smell

prey—an animal hunted by another animal for food

pup—a young shark

snout—the long front part of an animal's head; it includes the nose, mouth, and jaws

surface—the outside or outermost area of something

Read More

Barnes, Nico. *Great White Sharks.* Sharks. Minneapolis: Abdo Kids, 2015.

Meister, Cari. *Sharks.* Life Under the Sea. Minneapolis: Jump!, 2014.

Waxman, Laura Hamilton. *Great White Sharks.* Sharks. Mankato, Minn.: Amicus Ink, 2017.

Internet Sites

FactHound offers a safe, fun way to find Internet sites related to this book. All of the sites on FactHound have been researched by our staff.

Here's all you do:

Visit *www.facthound.com*

Type in this code: 9781515770022

 Check out projects, games and lots more at
www.capstonekids.com

Critical Thinking Questions

1. How do great white sharks catch seals?

2. What does a great white shark look like?

3. What is a nostril? How does a great white shark's nostrils help it catch prey?

Index